Mother and Baby
Zoo Animals

by Caroline Arnold   **photographs by Richard Hewett**

R
XZ
A

Carolrhoda Books, Inc./Minneapolis

Mother animals take
care of their babies.

A mother lion licks
her baby clean.

lions

A mother zebra
keeps her baby close
by her side.

The whole herd helps a mother elephant look after her baby.

A mother chimpanzee picks bugs and dirt from her baby's hairy coat.

chimpanzees

A mother flamingo watches over her baby in the nest.

A mother hippopotamus listens to her baby.

hippopotamuses

A mother panda
hugs her baby.

pandas

Penguin parents keep their baby's feathers neat and clean.

penguins

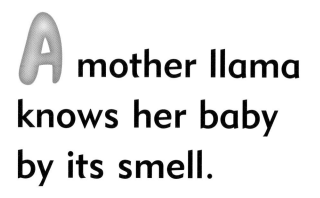A mother llama
knows her baby
by its smell.

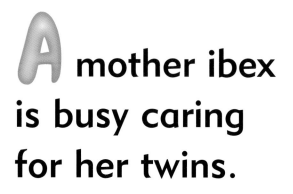A mother ibex
is busy caring
for her twins.

A mother orangutan gives her baby a piggyback ride.

orangutans

A mother kangaroo
keeps her baby
warm and snug
in her pouch.

kangaroos

Mother animals feed their babies and keep them safe until the babies can take care of themselves.

camels

Where can I find...

koalas

Caroline Arnold has written more than one hundred books for children. Many of the books are about animals. Caroline lives with her husband in Los Angeles, California.

Richard Hewett worked for magazines before he discovered children's books. He, too, has created many books about animals. Richard lives with his wife in Los Angeles, California.

This book is available in two bindings:
ISBN 1-57505-285-7 (lib. bdg.)
ISBN 1-57505-390-X (trade bdg.)

Carolrhoda Books, Inc., c/o The Lerner Publishing Group
241 First Avenue North, Minneapolis, MN 55401 U.S.A.

Website address: www.lernerbooks.com

Library of Congress Cataloging-in-Publication Data

Arnold, Caroline.
   Mother and baby zoo animals / by Caroline Arnold ; photographs by Richard Hewett.
      p.   cm.
   Includes index.
   Summary: Describes how mother zoo animals feed, clean, protect, and play with their babies.
   ISBN 1-57505-285-7 (lib. bdg.: alk. paper)
   1. Parental behavior in animals—Juvenile literature. 2. Zoo animals—Infancy—Juvenile literature. [1. Zoo animals—Infancy. 2. Zoo animals—Habits and behavior.]
I. Hewett, Richard, ill. II. Title.
QL762.A75   1999
591.56'3—dc21   98-15749

Manufactured in the United States of America
1 2 3 4 5 6 – JR – 04 03 02 01 00 99